THE YEAR OF 2022

Lockdowns in China, war in Europe

Nohad T. Harati

INTRODUCTION

Inflation proved to be persistent, especially after the invasion of Ukraine. The reversal of globalization and the tightening of labor markets seen during the pandemic were joined by new world challenges such as a hastening of the energy transition and an increase in defense budgets, adding extra burdens to government debt.

Monetary policy became a trial-and-error experiment. Considering this scenario, what level of interest rates would escape a recession or popular discontent, as reduced purchasing power was met with higher unemployment?

As shown in the following chapters, a shift from a low interest rate environment to an inflationary one is not a straightforward process as it demands accommodating new information and, in most cases, staying behind the curve.

By June, the orchestrated answer by central banks showed how much inflation expectations had taken over the economic debate. Meanwhile, Europe was shaken by political instability both inside the EU (Italy) as well as outside (UK).

On the backdrop of these troublesome times, climate change made itself noticeable through the heatwaves that swept across the old continent, bringing awareness of nature related problems that can soon impose difficult trade-offs in terms of global food supply.

The search for a new productivity boost proved to be the answer for greater economic growth as long as countries were able to implement proper public policies and, at the same time, maintain sound budgetary principles.

Unfortunately, tech darlings and other innovative businesses, crypto included, were facing difficulties of their own, greatly reducing their ability to contribute or even scale ideas to the next level.

CHAPTER 1

RAISING RATES

With the US facing higher inflation, the time to discuss interest rates had come.

Although disruptions caused by the pandemic were among the reasons for high prices, some elements prevail when it comes to monetary policy:

- A certain amount of time is required before its effects are felt in the economy
- Fossil fuel prices still impact inflation indices, regardless of the energy transition
- For the Fed, it is better to be ahead of the curve, raising rates gradually, than having to be more aggressive in the future
- Keeping rates low for longer encourages speculation, hurting small investors the most
- US interest rates affect the global economy

Other Times

Unlike the early 80s, when the US was struggling with stagflation by adopting nominal interest rates of 20%, rate hikes may represent the end of an economic cycle that stretched for a long period of time, which inevitably created some distortions.

One of them concerns quantitative easing (QE), a mechanism by which the central bank "creates" money to buy government bonds of various maturities, thus reducing their rates (the higher the price of a bond, the lower its yield).

From a fiscal point of view, its advantage lies in the fact that it is much cheaper for the government to finance itself by paying the interest charged on central bank reserves than in the many bond auctions carried out at market rates.

Despite being very useful to stimulate the economy when there is little room to reduce interest rates, it is believed that QE puts public debt at the mercy of short-term rates as it is reversed (a process known as "quantitative tightening" or "QT"), increasing financing costs.

In other words, the risk of rolling debt over increases, which in itself brings new problems.

As it can be observed, artificial situations only work when they have a temporary nature, reason why the Fed started discussing how soon it would reduce its balance sheet.

The Problem

Before the pandemic, asset prices in general were already at very high levels, providing an asymmetrical market with barely any chances of additional gains.

For the Fed, inflation was at an all-time high and unemployment was lower than in many parts of the world. Due to this more vigilant attitude, adjustments in asset prices were expected, as their cashflows are discounted at a higher rate.

Meanwhile, considering that the last decade was one of strength in the markets, a panic of great proportions had to be avoided, especially when taking into account the huge number of small investors that now participate.

After 2 years, the world had already adapted to the pandemic, meaning the secondary effects of so many stimulus policies had to be addressed.

Although markets have developed new instruments to prevent recessions as severe as the Great Depression of 1929, they are nowhere near to correcting the financial excesses that persistently show up when interest rates are kept low for longer.

CHAPTER 2

META STREET

Throughout 2020, it was common to mention the distinction between 2 worlds:
- "Wall Street" – the financial market, which greatly benefited from large-scale stimulus
- "Main Street" – the real economy, with people out of work and closed businesses

However, with interest rate rises on the horizon, as explained in the previous chapter, the focus then shifts to the differences between the real world and the virtual world ("Meta Street").

Real World

High inflation became the main global issue. In order to tame it, a truly independent central bank counts with only one monetary policy tool (interest rates).

When the cost of money rises, long-term interest rates follow, making financial assets adjust to the squeeze. The effects on the real economy, on the other hand, take longer to become visible and are harder to predict.

With governments, companies and individuals heavily leveraged, saying "goodbye" to the low interest rate economy was not that simple.

A macroeconomic fine tuning was thus necessary so that interest rates would fight inflation but not excessively burden all the agents that somehow depended on credit or whose assets were liquid enough as to lose value when financial conditions tighten.

All in an uncertain, post-pandemic environment.

Virtual World

Realizing that opportunities were beyond Main Street is what made Microsoft pay US$ 69 billion for Activision Blizzard, a games company. After all, it's not always that a global event keeps the entire planet stuck at home, with more time to play.

Improved headsets and other devices, which literally immersed individuals in a new world created with state-of-the-art chips, explains the metaverse race to the top. The aim is to monetize the 3D universe.

Considering the game world alone, the most popular of them (Fortnite) attracted 300 million users in just 4 years. Its appeal could not be greater. If people can attend concerts or even build an island, why not conduct economic activities there too?

It's not just another niche market. In 2021, the top five internet companies invested no less than US$ 149 billion in research and development, an amount bigger than the US Department of Defense's R&D budget.

Opportunity

The fact that Facebook abandoned the idea of launching its own currency, initially called Libra, did not prevent others from doing so in the virtual world. After all, decentralized finance (DeFi) allows payments and other financial transactions to be handled securely at a very low cost.

Hence, it's no wonder that companies are looking closer at

the world of games. While some seek a "share of mind", others are at a more advanced stage, selling their products as digital assets (NFTs).

Their trading is not limited to established brands. Anyone can create their own NFT collections, which in itself brings additional businesses.

Caveats

Nothing indicates that it will be a flawless process, starting with blockchain technology itself, which depends on clever computers solving mathematical problems to validate transactions. As more people make use of it, the greater the cost and time required to process them.

For now, any gains in scale imply giving up security or its decentralized nature. There is still no globally accepted standard, but it is believed that, due to its open source, improvements will eventually be added.

Another difficulty lies in the transit between the real world and the virtual world. In terms of products themselves, the challenge is creating a process where someone buys in the virtual world and receives it quickly at home. As for means of payment, the creation of a stablecoin.

Apparently, it can only be issued by regulated financial institutions. Therefore, the focus would go back to "Wall Street".

Brave New World

Big tech lives in a world with few restrictions.

With the internet in two dimensions, companies created and monetized social media, offering a wide range of services. Now, they aim a younger generation, that likes to shop in a virtual environment rich in tech resources.

Considering the gaming world alone, 2.8 billion people spend US$ 200 billion in a single year.

In a global economy with higher interest rates and slower growth, the companies of "Meta Street" are investing fortunes so that they don't stay behind. Regardless of the game they are playing, the truth is that technology has always been an inducer of productivity and profits, something that undoubtedly brings benefits, whether real or virtual.

CHAPTER 3

2022 VERSUS 2008

Although many are not aware of it, in financial markets everyone is connected to the same system. A debtor in one position might well be a creditor in another, making participants assess their risks as a whole rather than looking at each one individually.

As computer processing power became larger and cheaper, new financial instruments were created within this same system, allowing leverage to be shared by a greater number of agents.

Consequently, the role of financial markets has grown, encompassing a larger share of the economy.

2008

Throughout history, financial innovation has always occurred in times of low regulation.

As a benefit, financial products that accommodated different economic circumstances and needs. As a problem, the conflicts of interest that arose during the development and distribution of these products, a characteristic more related to people than to finances themselves.

It was no secret that banks used aggressive incentives, which meant that short-term goals led to practices that inevitably left the bill to investors or, in the worst case, to taxpayers.

Cyclical

Leverage has a cyclical nature. As financial assets grow during boom years, banks find no difficulty in lending more, which explains the crash that followed.

Since the 1970s that the following pattern became more common: more debt buys more assets which, in turn, guarantee new debt. This usually works well until the market runs out of new buyers.

Unlike other sectors of the economy, where lower prices attract new people, in the case of financial assets, lower prices reduce their value as collateral (guarantee), forcing agents to sell them to mitigate portfolio risk.

Once everyone starts doing the same, it's not hard to imagine the damage.

Rescue Plan

With the crisis in place, the world's main central bankers were called to act. Initially, there were doubts about the type of help needed. While the Fed expected a collapse, the rest worried about inflation.

The economic impact was so big that the dollar devalued to its lowest point since currencies once floated (1973), causing a jump in internationally quoted commodity prices.

Although high prices needed to be controlled globally, the Federal Reserve (Fed) was the only central bank with a dual mandate (price stability and full employment).

While trying to avoid a recession, resulting from an environment where houses were worth less, credit was scarce, food and fuel had become more expensive and job opportunities absent, the Germans, quite influential inside the European Central Bank (ECB), feared hyperinflation.

2022

As much as central bankers were grappling again with high inflation, financial markets were no longer the same as they were in 2008. Changes in regulation and technology have created a different system:
- Stricter rules inhibited risk-taking by banks
- Fintechs allowed trading for free, in addition to creating algorithms for decision making

Banks, despised by the Occupy Wall Street movement, have transferred the risks to other private agents and small investors who bought, among other things, shares and Exchange Traded Funds (ETFs).

Given the need to raise interest rates, were they prepared for a correction in prices?

Social Bubble

Robert Shiller, who won the Nobel Prize in Economics in 2013, studied the nature of financial bubbles. Making a comparison with the Great Depression of 1929, he highlights that, at that time, there was a lot of excitement around the financial market.

Relating to nowadays, it is a fact that GameStop and Nikola are the result of social media, something that started as an entertainment and that today influences investment decisions. As a result, it became harder to assess risks correctly.

For no other reason, the widespread belief that assets should be bought at each dip, even when they are still very expensive.

Bad Quality

When interest rates rise, "bad assets", which are just fads most of the time, suffer the most. That said, what really matters is how much market participants can handle before excesses are eliminated from the system.

It has been some time since banks got rid of their asset inventory, making it impossible for them to provide liquidity under stressful circumstances. Additionally, they register their derivatives with the same clearinghouses that served Robinhood, a startup forced to suspend its business last year.

Risk Takers

During the 2008 crisis, the world's leading central bankers pursued two goals:

1. Set interest rates more in line with a healthy economy
2. Address moral hazard, which incentivized recklessness

Currently, although through greater coordination, these objectives have become antagonistic: by raising interest rates to control inflation, the resulting excessive price correction would impact a larger group of people that trade through less regulated fintechs.

Roughly over a decade later, risks spread elsewhere. Given the implementation of the "Volcker rule", banks stopped trading on their own, working as service providers instead.

Today, everyone has an individual investment portfolio. As prices adjust to a new reality, it is a fact that there will be no central banker to save the legion of small investors who refused to see that the low interest rate party was coming to an end.

Risk is no longer on Wall Street. It's on everyone's smartphone.

CHAPTER 4

SANCTIONS

In the end of February, the unimaginable happens: Russia invades Ukraine.

Throughout history, European countries dealt with armed conflicts. However, the fight for international hegemony is no longer the same. With globalization and a widely interconnected financial system, foreign policy is now enforced through sanctions.

For nearly a decade, a third of the world's population has suffered their economic consequences, with Russia, the world's third largest oil producer, being the most recent case.

It's not the first time that happens. In 2014, the country was sanctioned for annexing Crimea, although to not such as big extent as now.

With the US, Britain and the European Union announcing measures ranging from the trading halt of Russian debt on international markets to the freezing of assets of individuals inside and outside of the Russian government, their families and businesses, what can be said about their impacts on the world economy, still recovering from the economic effects of the pandemic?

Sanction Origins

In order to maintain peace after the end of World War I, Europe was subject to strong sanctions. Hence, its first characteristic: sanctions are not applied unilaterally. A group of countries come together to punish who doesn't play by the same rules and could eventually declare war.

This punishment for misconduct used to be enforced by blocking the access to basic supplies or by prohibiting businesses with certain countries. Over the years, the strategy evolved. Governments began to include economists in the discussions, so that sanctions also covered how certain activities were financed.

However, the desired outcomes were not always achieved. The financial system changed and, as more important countries became targets, it was more difficult to maintain a minimum level of cooperation between nations, which then became increasingly protectionist.

Common Targets

Among the most exposed sectors are finances, technology, and energy.

After the terrorist attack of September 11 (2001), which toppled the twin towers in New York, the US government passed the Patriot Act, allowing for the confiscation of funds that financed such activities.

Over time, regulation was fine-tuned to include a larger group of people, such as dictators, limiting their access to the US dollar-based international financial system, controlled by Washington D.C.

In the meantime, banks were held accountable for monitoring and blocking the funds of individuals, companies and countries included in the US government's "black list". As a result, the costs and fines paid by these financial intermediaries sky-rocketed.

Upgrades

In 2010, the US added the so-called secondary sanctions, which prohibited companies from doing business with targets that match the Patriot Act. That's when the technology sector got its first hit as cell phones and other consumer goods also became eligible.

Energy, the last sector of the three mentioned before, is perhaps the most complicated one, especially when considering the chaos seen in commodity markets in 2021. For energy companies themselves, sanctions affect not only the production of oil and gas, but also limits financing, making it impossible for them to raise funds through financial markets.

Even US and European oil companies found trouble, once taken into account some notorious cross-shareholdings in Russian companies:
- BP owned approximately 20% of Rosneft
- Shell, just over 25% of a Gazprom gas project
- Exxon explored oil and gas together with two Rosneft subsidiaries

Similar cases applied to trading companies, based in neutral jurisdictions such as Switzerland, which financed themselves with European banks in order to establish partnerships in Russian projects that supplied Europe with natural gas.

Bypass

Countries exposed to sanctions often look for alternatives, such as other currencies or financial hubs to maintain their activities.

In Russia's case, the US dollar represented approximately

half of its US$430 billion in reserves in 2017. Two years later, that percentage dropped to 22% as the Russian central bank opted for a larger share of euros and yuans (China's currency).

For sanctioned parties, containing the initial damage is always the hardest part. In 2018, when the Trump administration applied sanctions against two Russian oligarchs and their respective aluminum companies, the ruble (local currency) devalued and chaos reached the London Metal Exchange (LME), where the metal was traded.

Donald Trump was, by far, the president that used this practice the most, apparently with infinite creativity. Back then, Russia defended itself by issuing sovereign debt in euros, and by asking Russian companies to list their shares on the local exchange, allowing them to also trade in other currencies.

Looking ahead, the impacts of generalized sanctions may jeopardize the energy transition, as copper and nickel, inputs used for the production of batteries, are geographically concentrated. This is due to the fact that important countries can retaliate or reduce their dependency on the international financial system, replacing their US dollar reserves with other currencies.

Broadly speaking, the more indiscriminate the use of sanctions, the worse the results. As the month of March started, the world went back to chaos mode.

CHAPTER 5

REDRAWING THE MAP

The prices of oil (Brent and WTI) rose well above US$ 100 after the invasion of Ukraine, while the Russian ruble collapsed, partly due to the resistance of the Ukrainians, and partly due to the number of sanctions applied to Russia.
The sale of Premier League's Chelsea and the seizure of Russian oligarchs' luxury yachts in European marinas were some showcase curiosities, highlighting the international connections of businesses and the global fortunes amassed during the golden age of globalization.

Planned War

Political scientists mentioned time and again that the conflict between Russia and Ukraine was just a matter of time. Putin's instinct identified weaknesses in some of the world's major economies, which favored the timing for the attack:
- A prime minister likely to fall in the UK
- A French president on the eve of an election
- A German government with a different arrangement (the end of the Merkel era)
- A US government looking for a common enemy after the disastrous exit from Afghanistan

Ukraine has not had a pro-Russian regime since 2014, which reduced Putin's influence in countries that were once part of the Soviet Union and that have since joined the North Atlantic Treaty Organization (NATO), a Western military alliance.

Feeling threatened, Russia intended, with its so-called "special military operation", to appoint a new president who, obviously, would not have the legitimacy to run the country. This explains why it became increasingly isolated.

Fortress Russia

With the collapse of the USSR in 1991, Russia faced inflation levels above 2,000%.

Seven years later, it defaulted on its international debt, as its currency devalued by more than 60%. As a major oil exporter, it suffered the consequences of the end of the commodity super cycle. Its economy went downhill.

This led to the construction of what became "Fortress Russia". In order to ensure its self-sufficiency, it diversified its economy away from oil and gas. In addition, it increased its business partners and technology providers.

Regarding the country's finances, it reduced its foreign debt, adopted a very restrictive fiscal and monetary policy, while accumulating international reserves (US$ 630 billion, or something close to 40% of GDP).

This would have been enough to maintain stability in local markets were it not for the large number of international funds, representing institutional investors, that participated in it through exchange traded funds (ETFs).

Black Swan Event

With all the bragging about clever algorithms, the financial community still struggles to adequately price extreme events such as wars, pandemics, and climate change, which explains why many were stuck with Russian assets in their portfolios.

Excluded from the international network that processes payments between financial institutions (SWIFT), Fortress Russia faced difficulties in honoring commitments to banks, bondholders, companies, and shareholders, causing everyone to simultaneously hold assets that were worth much less than previously thought.

That 70'S Show

It is impossible to dissociate Russia's decision to go to war from its impact on world inflation. At a price of US$ 150 per oil barrel, global growth would be reduced by 1.6% while world inflation would increase by much more (2%).

That would be enough to throw the world economy back to 1973, when another war led to the first oil shock of the 1970s. Central bankers, however, still thought higher energy prices were temporary, mainly to avoid the same mistakes made by the European Central Bank (ECB) which, by raising rates in 2008 and 2011, sent the continent off the rails.

The challenge was to stop prices that were already rising at a fast pace even before the war started, albeit under different circumstances.

On the American side of the planet, there were concerns about the effects of the increase in interest rates on asset prices. On the European side, the resistance to raising them, given the expectation of low growth in the face of even more expensive natural gas.

Like the lockdowns imposed by governments when the pandemic hit, this context of great uncertainty would last longer than initially anticipated.

CHAPTER 6

COLLATERAL DAMAGE

When it comes to geopolitics, it is a fact that when a country is unable to access its international reserves, there is little it can do to defend its currency and, more broadly, its economy.

Taking into account the most recent conflict in Europe, what would have been the alternatives for Russia, under harsh and widespread sanctions? Much of the diplomatic discussions focused on the kind of solutions China could provide in terms of energy purchases, new export opportunities, as well as international payment systems, all of which with their own limitations.

Reality Shock

Regardless of the type of weaponry (whether military or financial), the truth is that much of the predicted scarcity in the world was still a number on a commodity exchange screen back then, not having reached the real economy yet.

A peculiarity of the European conflict was the sharp rise in agricultural commodity prices. Both Ukraine and Russia were major food exporters. For that reason, the price of wheat rose 30% in a period of only 2 weeks. To plant it, farmers already had paid more for the natural gas used to produce the fertilizer.

With the war, production from Ukraine was no longer accessible while output from Russia was unavailable. Not because there were direct sanctions against food coming from Russia, but because companies feared secondary sanctions for doing business with the country or transporting goods without any form of insurance.

In order to guarantee food security, it is very common for other countries to reduce or ban exports altogether, aware that they may face additional losses in future harvests when climate change is taken into account.

As Russia advanced militarily, it became obvious that the impacts of the war on the world economy will be felt for a long time. On the economic front, the strategy of freezing assets abroad put into doubt the use of international reserves as a hedge against external shocks, given that they become unavailable at the exact moment they should be deployed.

Nonetheless, it is a fact that there is no substitute for the US dollar as a world reserve currency. Individuals and companies can switch their wealth into cryptocurrencies, but it is very unlikely that countries would do so, subjecting themselves to an additional list of factors that they do not control.

In the past, high food prices led to protests in North Africa and the Middle East, a region that imports and subsidizes much of the food it consumes in order to cushion the impacts of inflation that comes from abroad. The result was the Arab Spring.

CHAPTER 7

MYTHS AND FACTS

The invasion of Ukraine also accelerated a few trends.

The first of them being the reversal of globalization. The formation of regional economic blocs had been a reality since Donald Trump started to impose tariffs on international trade as a foreign policy tool.

Country leaders, more broadly, did not want to depend on governments that didn't share the same vision. As a result, a more divided world and less economic growth, which was also true for China.

All for the sake of guaranteeing energy, technology and other relevant supplies, elements that would define the composition of international reserves for any nation, whether on the basis of trade interests or geopolitical relations.

Digital Currencies

Regardless of what aspect predominated in this war, one of the myths is the loss of the dollar's status as a reserve currency.

As much as it is claimed that this system is imperfect for benefiting the US too much, it is necessary to understand the dynamics of international transactions:

- 39.92% of international payments are made in dollars
- 36.56% of international payments are made in euros

By countries holding reserves in the following currencies:

- 59.15% in dollars
- 20.48% in euros

The Winter Olympics, which served as a stage for the launch of the digital yuan, did not expose what happened behind the scenes: for a greater international acceptance, China would have to abandon all forms of capital controls, a political decision that would take into account the next topic.

Energy Transition

In the short term, some factors are decisive for energy commodities.

Given the restrictions imposed on Russia, an increase in oil supply depended on a response from OPEC, the US shale sector or China's zero tolerance policy towards covid-19.

On the cartel's part, Saudi Arabia and the United Arab Emirates (UAE) could compensate for the imbalance. On the US side however, the increase in interest rates, added to ESG concerns, made it impossible to finance an activity that otherwise would greatly benefit from production flexibility.

The fact that China was still imposing lockdowns reduced demand equivalent to Venezuela's oil production, but it was somewhat naive to imagine that an agreement signed by the European Union with the US would totally eliminate the dependence on autocratic governments like the one commanded by the Kremlin.

Considering the goals imposed to fight global warming, 70% of energy generation will have to come from renewable sources in a period not exceeding three decades, multiplying exponentially the demand for cobalt, copper, and nickel.

Geographic Concentration

As it is the case for oil and gas, the reserves of these metals are geographically concentrated, which brings new global dilemmas.

When oil and, to a lesser extent, gas began to replace coal in the G7 countries, their proportion in the energy matrix also followed a similar pattern, rising from 26% to around 70%.

For no other reason, the enrichment of the so-called "petrostates", many of which are located in the Middle East. Even with the energy transition, the idea of a world free of fossil fuels is nothing but a myth.

There would then be a delicate geopolitical balance between two groups:

1. Low-cost oil producers, with the aggravating factor that they would increase their market share to 57%
2. Rising countries, with the potential to become "electrostates"

Green Curse

With the climate emergency knocking on the door, meeting the desired quantities is one of the big challenges. New mines take more than a decade to become operational, and since the end of the China-led commodity super cycle, companies have stopped investing.

This means that miners would face two scenarios:

1. Mines with reserves of inferior quality, increasing their production costs
2. Mines in unstable economies, where problems tend to aggravate as they become reliant on a single commodity ("commodity curse")

Recent history is littered with cases of countries burying their export sectors as their currencies appreciated ("Dutch disease") or over-leveraging during the bonanza.

With Russia's central bank reserves frozen, a global debate began on whether commodities could replace a system based on the US currency and US bonds.

Taking into account the energy sector, geopolitics will be realigned according to trade agreements that grant access to certain metals, partially replacing the current flow of petrodollars.

On the side of democratic economies, Australia stands out, along with Chile, with large lithium and copper reserves. On the opposite side, Congo, with almost half of the global cobalt reserves and China, with aluminum, copper, and lithium reserves.

The scenario for global growth, 2 years after the pandemic, could not have been bleaker. With higher energy and food prices, many countries chose to substantially reduce their imports which, together with higher interest rates, promised to jeopardize any consistent world recovery.

It is yet to be seen if a new economic order can replace the old one, without repeating the same mistakes.

CHAPTER 8

COLD WAR 2.0

The war in Ukraine became increasingly brutal.

More than imposing another round of sanctions, governments found themselves with another, equally important task: write policies encouraging companies to invest in clean energy while juggling the geopolitical risks of gas supplying countries.

In the meantime, high inflation rates had already spread across the world.

Fed's Response

An abrupt interest rate change. In addition, the announcement of the beginning of the reduction of the Fed's balance sheet in the month of May.

For anyone following the US economy, it became clear that the Federal Reserve had finally woken up. It is a fact that the invasion of Ukraine had its contribution in raising prices of essential goods, but the Americans were already in an atypical situation even before the war.

In the jobs market, there were twice as many open positions. If in the past salary negotiations were based on the fight for talent, the predominant theme became the rapid increase in the cost of living.

The Fed's track record for a "soft landing" of the economy was never the best. On only 3 occasions, over a period of approximately 80 years, was it able to adjust macroeconomic conditions without wreaking havoc.

Balance Reduction

Quantitative easing (or "QE") was still unconventional after the 2008 crisis. Since then, it became so routine that it was turbocharged at the beginning of the pandemic, given its objectives:

- Keep interest rates low, including long-term ones
- Give liquidity to the markets, allowing them to function well even in adverse conditions

Over the course of a decade or so, QE inflated asset prices, causing the well-known distinction between "Main Street" and "Wall Street". Even privately issued cryptocurrencies had their go in the meantime.

Considering the high levels of inflation worldwide, the time had come to do just the opposite. Until then, that was tried only once: in 2019, the year the Fed stopped reinvesting bonds as they matured, effectively reducing its asset stock.

Given the need to act, the process had to be implemented faster. While the interest rate pace set by the Fed had its effect on the economy somewhat known, the same was not true about the impacts of reducing the balance sheet on long-term rates.

For some economists at the Massachusetts Institute of Technology (MIT), they could be far greater.

Central Bank Digital Currencies

Theoretically, such dilemmas could be addressed through currencies issued by central banks (CBDC).

Throughout history, the way money circulates in the economy has alternated between 2 models:

- Centralized, under the control of a central bank;
- Decentralized, through the infrastructure developed by banks and financial institutions.

Although the first model had predominated, it was highly unlikely to go to the other extreme after years of monetary stimuli. That said, digital currencies issued by governments will still be relevant, with others, also regulated, circulating around them.

This hybrid model would thus be subject to some risks, depending on the choices on:
- Technology
- Security of individual data

Business Model Rethink

Central banks' credibility would remain essential, regardless of whether the currency is physical or digital. However, the way in which they implement it determines growth, employment, and inflation.

As an example, stimuli in recessionary periods, through the adoption of negative interest rates, would change their way of functioning: instead of banks suffering from withdrawals, the central bank itself would induce the desired behavior, causing people to spend more.

With this direct relationship between the central bank and the population, commercial banks, mere intermediaries between savers and debtors, would need a rethink about their business models.

Would they keep accounts with a balance above a certain threshold? Or would they be in charge for implementing a dual account system (CBDC and conventional bank account), exploiting the digital data provided by the former in order to offer financial services through the latter?

Risk Management

Regardless of the role played by banks, regulators around the world are contemplating the use of blockchain technology in order to improve risk management within the international financial system.

As cryptocurrency trading takes place around the clock, this automated infrastructure allows the real-time monitoring of risks, which would theoretically reduce the chances of market participants being caught in the day after of a financial explosion (like that of Archegos Capital Management) or an attack on a neighboring country (like it is the case for China and Taiwan).

21St Century Cold War

The consequences of the war in Ukraine were felt everywhere and the conflict was far from over. As Russian diplomats were expelled from many countries, Finland, a country that shares its border with Russia, began its application process for NATO membership.

The Fed hiked interest rates as Europe grappled with more expensive energy prices, in a context where China was still closed for business.

Gone are the days when economies acted in sync, which can hamper the international coordination needed to implement and connect the emerging new energy and finance infrastructures.

This is what the Cold War of the 21st century looked like.

CHAPTER 9

THE FUTURE OF THE EURO

The presidential election in France was surrounded by some curious facts:
- Low voter participation (38.5% of the total of valid votes)
- A second term for the current president (Emmanuel Macron), something that hasn't happened for 2 decades
- A second term for a president with a parliamentary majority, unheard of since 1965

Re-elections have been uncommon since the 2000 referendum reduced the presidential term from 7 to 5 years, given the broad powers granted to the position. In France, the president is responsible for external affairs, such as declaring war, and internal ones, such as appointing ministers and dissolving the National Assembly.

Although the opponent (Marine Le Pen) lost again, albeit by a smaller difference, the election result shows why, 2 years into the pandemic and with a war inside the continent, the French voted for the "status quo".

2017

When Macron, unknown to the political world, launched himself as a candidate representing a newly formed party (La République en Marche – LREM), populism was taking hold. Brexit, decided a year earlier, was accompanied by Donald Trump's victory in the US.

In many parts of Europe, radical governments promised to abandon the euro and the entire legal and institutional framework behind the European Union (EU). For no other reason, concerns about the elections in France, second largest economy within the block.

Open For Business

Given his experience (Macron is a former investment banker), his speech was based on the defense of globalization. Training for the 21st century and a business-friendly environment were top priorities.

Once elected, he reshaped the tax system, reducing corporate taxes and changing income and financial transaction taxes, as well as attracting foreign investors. This has allowed the country to form its own group of unicorns, companies with valuations above US$1 billion.

During his first term, he used France's heft on the continent to advance on Europe's integration which, given the lack of a common budget, is still considered unfinished, roughly two decades after the launch of the euro.

Macron, who shares the same nationality as Christine Lagarde, president of the European Central Bank (ECB), is credited for bringing into life the €750 billion fund created to help economies inside the EU most affected by the pandemic.

Very shrewd in his geopolitical vision, Macron understood well the risks posed by "China" and "Putin".

Quoi Qu'il En Coûte

Considering that France adopts the welfare state model, it

spent accordingly to avoid the worst when the economy was locked down at the beginning of 2020. A series of programs were put in place, for the most diverse purposes:
- An additional €150 for people who had some type of benefit
- Up to €650 of additional payment to healthcare professionals
- €1 limit price for meals at universities
- Free breakfast at schools located in poor areas

Government support also included aid for companies so that people would remain employed.

Although modest when compared to the US, the response lived up to the term "whatever the cost", being superior than the total spent by Scandinavian countries, known for their extensive social protection systems.

As a result, French GDP had already returned to pre-pandemic levels in 2021.

President Of The Rich

Given his short term, Macron was unable to address some issues, which ended up benefiting Marine Le Pen.

Similar to the UK, the cosmopolitan elite of Paris clashed with the rest of France. While managing the country as a M&A (mergers and acquisitions) project, he faced some very unpopular tasks, such as raising the retirement age.

The minimum age for men is 60 years old. Being lower than the average in other European countries, Macron was forced to put aside plans to overhaul the existing 42 programs when the pandemic hit.

For no other reason, Le Pen brilliantly explored this theme, along with the rising cost of living (inflation), the side effect of a series of lockdown induced supply shocks and the war in Ukraine than from mismanagement itself.

Once election results were known, the euro slightly appreciated, as uncertainty abated. France is among the most indebted countries in the EU, together with the usual spendthrifts (Greece and Italy). Its deficit exceeds 7% while its public debt is around 115% of GDP.

Even when taking into account the latest stimulus programs, figures are very far from the Maastricht Treaty rules, which limited deficits to 3% of GDP and public debt to 60% of GDP.

As they became more flexible over the years to accommodate different countries and periods of slow growth, they largely explain the devaluation of the euro. If there is one thing that lacks consensus among member states is what fiscal policy should be like.

As far as Macron's country is concerned, although its decent economic performance favors the financing of its public debt, it will be very difficult to reduce it without a plan and some political will.

It remains to be seen whether his pragmatic way of doing things will work again. This is what France, the European Union and, fundamentally, the euro depend on.

CHAPTER 10

LOST DECADE

A period in which countries barely grow, face a series of financial crises, and struggle with popular discontent.

As much as it is known that economies have a cyclical nature, it is rather bumpy when it comes to emerging countries, as history shows:
- Between the 60's and 70's, this group grew tremendously
- Between the 80's and 90's, they dealt with the so-called "lost decade"
- Towards the turn of the century, they resumed growth, mainly due to China

More recently, with the Federal Reserve tightening and the reversal of globalization, are these economies doomed to another lost decade?

As it was the case for 2022, thanks to a period of extremely low interest rates around the world, debt levels were quite high when the US raised rates to combat the inflationary effects of the oil shocks of the 1970s (1973 and 1979).

The Lost Decade

Emerging countries usually have, at varying degrees, one or more of the following:
- High government intervention in the economy, either through a large number of state-owned companies or through its level of spending when compared to GDP

- Years of high inflation, resulting from public debt mismanagement (the cost of social programs vis-à-vis a high informal sector that pays no taxes)
- Currency intervention and capital controls
- Commodity-based exports
- Low level of domestic savings, when considering investment opportunities

Consequently, they are financed by:
- Official loans: provided by entities such as the World Bank
- Bank loans: contracts where foreign banks lend directly to countries
- Bonds: issuance and sale of fixed income securities in international markets
- Foreign direct investments: such as when a new factory is built by a foreign company
- Portfolio investments: very common when government companies are sold or in countries with more developed capital markets

Between 1982 and 1983, many Latin American countries defaulted on their foreign debt, taken mainly with US banks that recycled Arab petrodollars.

With the sharp increase in interest rates promoted by the US, the world economy was already in recession 2 years before. Most countries navigated an adverse scenario:
- An increase in the amount of interest they paid
- A devaluation of their currencies
- Barely any international demand for their exports

As a result, runaway inflation and public spending cuts.

Mexico was the first to declare that it had exhausted its international reserves, cutting off the flow of loans to other countries in the region. Poverty increased as the minimum wage, in real terms, lost a third of its value.

Meanwhile, in the US, the International Monetary Fund (IMF), together with local banks, sought a coordinated solution, thus avoiding a blow up of the international financial system.

Washington Consensus

With the Washington Consensus, Latin American economies adopted a new model. Despite technically better, it was far from perfect since:
- It favored the sale of state-owned companies, without contemplating a minimum legal framework to guarantee a competitive environment
- It affected the value of currencies, without addressing the side effects
- It did not include the creation of social safety nets, something of extreme importance for countries under development

However, by and large, the region's economies came out stronger.

Quantitative Tightening

Going back to 2022, a 3% increase in a single year is something the Fed has not done since the early 1990s.

Worse than having to pay more for a bigger pile of debts is the fact that countries do not deal with a single group of creditors any more. Today, any renegotiation would be much more complex as China plays a big role in infrastructure project funding.

This makes it all the more difficult to agree on a plan and gather public support for it, as the population suffers an increasingly explosive combination of rationing and high inflation. Social and, consequently, political instability does not match with favorable loan conditions.

Once deprived of financing and some flexibility to export more and better, it is a fact that emerging countries, despite having increased their international reserves, will still be exposed to the lost decade trap.

CHAPTER 11

STABLECOINS

The crypto market was always seen as an alternative to the limitations of the traditional financial system. After just over a decade of much liquidity, creativity ran wild, whether in cryptocurrencies' design, whether in the names used.

Until then, they seemed to be the perfect solution for governments that printed too much money, greedy bankers or for addressing inequality, given that many saw them as business opportunities.

Broadly, this ecosystem developed around the following:

1. Technology enthusiasts, who created their own currencies
2. Infrastructure providers, with their massive processing power computers
3. Exchanges, that benefited from anything that could be traded, without the obligation to provide any guarantees to investors
4. Small investors, in charge of turning the wheel

Looking at the participants above, it is not difficult to relate to the investment banks, stock exchanges, brokers, and investors who allocate part of their money to more traditional financial market products were it not for a slight detail: the absence of a basic asset to back the whole system.

Algorithm

The uproar faced by cryptocurrencies in mid-May was not due to any new information about the war in Ukraine or hawkish comments on monetary policy by the Federal Reserve (Fed) or the European Central Bank (ECB).

Something similar to a virtual bank run shook Terraform Labs, responsible for a market until then valued at US$ 40 billion and based on a supposedly US dollar stablecoin (TerraUSD), and a cryptocurrency (Luna).

An algorithm calibrated the relationship between the two. For every unit of stablecoin issued, the equivalent of $1 of Luna had to be "burned" (taken out of circulation).

Volatility

In the crypto world, nothing yet meets the third requirement of a currency (store of value) or makes their acceptance mandatory, which explains much of the volatility.

In addition, nothing determines their intrinsic value, since they do not have any future cashflows of returns (such as interest payments or dividends) or any other type of income. In that case, it is easy for them to succumb to large sale orders, especially if accompanied by negative comments on Twitter.

Small investors, holders of crypto assets, respond by panicking. On the other hand, an algorithm makes no judgement calls and acts by doing exactly as programmed: by issuing more cryptocurrencies, which consequently become less valuable.

The result of both is a virtual contagion, as other, theoretically stronger coins are sold in an attempt to contain the damage. How much these also suffer in the process is due, again, to the quality of their asset-backing.

Tether

Tether, the largest of stablecoins, did not provide enough details on that matter, as it was never a regulated business.

In the past, many had pointed out to the risky strategy by which it ensured its parity with the US dollar: cash and US treasury bonds made up only 5% of its total assets.

Regular audits are a rarity, making it difficult to separate the winners from the losers. Regardless of that, cryptos have a strong positive correlation with the stock markets, with the aggravating factor of lower liquidity.

Faced with the risk-off mode that had taken hold of tech shares, what other factors could give cryptos any boost? Usually, founders support their "offspring" in times of distress, but that doesn't always solve the problem.

Coinbase

At the time of Coinbase's IPO, it was thought that a crypto exchange, traded on a traditional exchange, could act as a gateway to the launching of crypto assets.

As a regulated entity, it meets the requirements imposed by the Securities and Exchange Commission (SEC). In the same way, it follows US laws applicable to publicly traded companies.

That said, it didn't take long for one document, among the many companies are obliged to file, to cause discomfort by informing that investors could lose their crypto assets held in the exchange.

It was a disclaimer, the kind of information few people read, that made explicit what commitments would be honored first if Coinbase ran into trouble.

Gyen

For non-regulated assets, there is no mechanism that transfers investors holdings to another institution or even some form of insurance, as it happens to be the case for bank deposits.

This is exactly what GYEN investors discovered. The stablecoin, allegedly pegged to the Japanese yen, had its trading suspended by Coinbase after losing 80% of its value on a single day.

So much for exchanges that brag about being open for trading 24 hours a day, 7 days a week.

Stablecoins, acting as a link between the traditional market and the crypto market, brought many concerns to financial agents worried about financial contagion.

It is undeniable that losses in the virtual world are offset by the sale of more conventional investments that are, in one way or another, in everyone's portfolio (such as Exchange Traded Funds - ETFs). In other circumstances, they would not be bothered by algorithm failures, for example.

As much as there is a wonderful technology (blockchain) out there, cryptocurrencies are seen with reservations, as they are even used to pay for illegal activities. This only increases the pressure for some form of supervision, considering its speculative nature and the lack of a minimum set of international rules.

The truth is that nothing holds by itself for too long.

CHAPTER 12

TURN ON A DIME

On June 7th, Australia's central bank raised its benchmark interest rates by 0.50%. A few days later, the European Central Bank (ECB) announced its expectation for the euro zone: successive interest rate hikes, the first being 0.25% in July.
The Federal Reserve (Fed) intensified its tightening to 0.75% at its June 15th meeting, followed by the central bank of Brazil, which raised the rate by another 0.50%. The next day, other monetary authorities followed suit, culminating in a 0.50% increase by the Swiss central bank, a first since 2007.
Going back in time, few imagined this orchestrated move among central bankers. Until then, it was believed that the Fed was in the process of announcing a smaller increase, while the ECB had just announced the end of its asset purchase program.

Out Of Control

For anyone who followed the press conference shortly after the Fed's decision, two things were clear:
1. The impossible task of accommodating supply to demand, given China's "zero tolerance" policy towards covid-19 and its respective lockdowns
2. How much the impacts of the war in Ukraine affected inflation expectations.

In the case of Europe specifically, a third element outside of its control had to be added: the budgets of EU member countries and their debt levels.

For no other reason the emergency meeting held at the time, as European sovereign bond rates began to drift. The end of the asset purchase program meant the return of some old ghosts.

What would be the fate of heavily indebted countries in face of such a troubled scenario?

An Unfinished Project

The European Union is still a work in progress. A central bank (ECB) is responsible for monetary policy while each member country sets its own fiscal policy, defining how much each pays to finance itself.

In the hierarchy of sovereign European bonds traded on the secondary market, rates are nothing more than the spread over a benchmark (the return paid by Germany's bond, the most liquid and the safest bond in the region).

In a context of rising interest rates, the greater the monetary tightening, the greater the spread shown by certain sovereign bonds, indicating 2 risks: the risk of a country defaulting or, worse, abandoning the euro.

As beneficial as a monetary union may be, this possibility exists due to the effects that interest rate differences can cause, making credit more expensive for companies and families, which can foster a popular desire for resurrecting national currencies.

Inflation Expectations

Throughout the year, central bankers appeared to be more in line with the work of Jeremy Rudd, researcher at the Fed.

Unlike the economic wisdom that claims that expectations are what determine inflation, he argued that real prices were what mattered, thus triggering generalized pass-throughs.

Although there were concerns about a repetition of the 1970s pattern, where higher wages led to higher prices (wage-price spiral), it was important to remember how globalization and the loss of union representation reduced the power over wages.

Another structural factor added to the debate over how prices manifest themselves in the economy was the shift in global supply chains. It is a fact that the pandemic and an armed conflict had reshaped the way capital and labor are used.

The production efficiency seen in regions with cheaper inputs and/or labor was replaced by greater diversification of suppliers, together with the formation of safety inventories.

The term "just-in-time" had fallen into disuse, giving way to "just in case".

Another trend in this search for self-sufficiency and consequent regionalization was the verticalization of production, where a company controls all of its stages, giving it greater pricing power.

Over time, central banks refuted the idea that they should consider other purposes. They rather kept their mandate unchanged (price stability and low unemployment, when considering the Fed) through the use of a single tool (interest rates). To this end, they acted gradually, showing clarity and predictability.

Admittedly, economies behaved under new rules, the effects of which were not immediately noticeable, increasing the degree of uncertainty. On the one hand, a sequence of supply shocks influenced prices on a global scale. On the other, a different post-pandemic job market, where vacancies were filled through zoom, regardless of geographic location.

Given this scenario, the need for change became clear. Agility had gained utter importance.

CHAPTER 13

REGIONALIZATION

Looking strictly at the economic side and, not considering climate change, it is believed that the following elements will definitely shape the world order:
- The disarray in global supply chains since the beginning of the pandemic
- The sanctions resulting from a war in Europe
- The effects of US monetary policy

Since then, a few theories emerged, not always with the proper fundamentals.

Rise Of Cryptocurrencies

The first theory considered the possibility of cryptocurrencies becoming a relevant part of flows that cross borders, given their low cost, security and lack of any government interference.

Sovereign digital currencies and the decrease in rampant speculation observed in the middle of the year put to rest any progress in this direction, even though part of the technological infrastructure (blockchain) may yet have practical applications for the international financial system.

Fall Of The Us Dollar

A second theory, that the dollar would lose its status as an international currency, stemmed from the application of sanctions, with the additional risk of increasing defaults. Any agent, be it an individual, a company or a country with dollar assets is for sure exposed to what is decided in Washington D.C.

Additionally, the dollar's role as the world's reserve currency brings another issue: the fact that the world is subject to US interest rates, affecting emerging countries in general and creating other monetary policy responses across the planet.

Considering these circumstances, a regionalization would make sense to fight the ubiquitous dollar, but that would come with costs. For any new arrangements, where more politically aligned countries would try to guarantee self-sufficiency and some degree of influence, the European Union (EU) brings some lessons.

Joining The Club

Originally composed of Belgium, France, Germany, Italy, Luxembourg and the Netherlands, the group expanded, encompassing increasingly different countries.

It was during this period of integration that Europe became rich. The United Kingdom, which was a member until early 2020 ("Brexit"), joined in 1973. Countries such as Spain, Portugal and Greece became members in the 1980s. Finland and Sweden, in talks to join NATO, have been members since 1995.

In the 2000s, the EU took its development model to countries in Eastern Europe, filling the space left by the fall of the former Soviet Union, while aiming at maintaining peace. Croatia was the last one to be accepted, in 2013.

As it grew, its territorial extent became a politically sensitive issue. In the same way that it brought some sort of stability to the continent, it was also prone to new problems.

Finland's border with Russia, Kaliningrad and the Turkish side of Cyprus (despite having applied for membership, Turkey is not part of the EU) showed the limits of the regionalization proposed by Europe.

Requirements

The extensive membership list, which at one point reached 28 nations, hides the long and arduous process of joining the club.

Initially, the application requires unanimous approval. For Ukraine specifically, it would represent the fifth largest population within the group (44 million Ukrainians), although with a much lower economic weight.

Negotiations start as soon as a country gains "candidate" status, moment in which it needs to adapt its laws to the EU's extensive legal framework, known as the "acquis communautaire".

Divided into several parts, it ranges from agricultural subsidy (which impacts countries like Ukraine) to the free movement of labor and the social benefits to be provided. To become a member, it is hence necessary to excel in all aspects.

Among other things, the implementation of democracy and the rule of law, in addition to a free-market economy capable of competing with other countries inside the EU, including in environmental aspects.

The Euro

The adoption of the euro, which implies in austerity measures such as those defined by the Maastricht Treaty (deficits limited to 3% of GDP and public debt limited to 60% of GDP) and adjustments in the banking system, is normally left for the end, occasion on which the new member can enjoy currency stability and low interest rates.

The process ends with the ratification by all member countries, which includes the legislative formalities of each and, in some cases, approval by the population, which needs strong incentives considering what is then required by Brussels.

What can be learned from the European experience is that some flexibility or even a transitory period is advisable, reason why some countries choose to maintain their own currencies. Instead of years of difficulties and demands, a process where benefits are granted gradually.

Understanding some principles and implementing what has already been tested are great ways to organize and boost regional economies. Anything beyond that, such as a privately issued cryptocurrency as part of central bank reserves or a new international currency replacing the US dollar, makes absolutely no sense.

CHAPTER 14

ITALY'S DOOM LOOP

The European Central Bank (ECB) joined other central banks in July, although it decided for a larger initial increase (of 0.50%) in interest rates.

That was made possible because of the Transmission Protection Instrument (TPI), yet another set of letters in ECB's arsenal. Its aim was to avoid rising financing costs for any EU member country, something that could force it to abandon the euro.

Monetary Firefighters

Even if not mentioned directly, it was a way of addressing the political instability in Italy. Third largest economy in the bloc, it could face serious problems, given its high debt levels in a forced activity slowdown due to the reduction of Russian gas supply in the continent.

Under TPI, the ECB would have discretion to buy not only sovereign debt (issued by countries) but also private debt (issued by companies), deviating from previous programs in which it purchased sovereign bonds in accordance with the economic importance of each country.

All to stop what the central bank considered an unjustified and disorderly reaction of the markets.

Doom Loop

The ability of a highly indebted country to honor its

financial commitments is always put to the test. As the previous euro crisis showed, nearly a decade ago, Italian banks had a high exposure to their own government debt.

When its accounts are compromised, it shakes the finances of the local banks, exposing them to the need of financial rescue by the same government already in difficulties. The cycle, called the "doom loop", feeds itself as bank credit is reduced, slowing down the economy and, consequently, government revenues.

Unlike the US and its thriving capital markets, Europe is highly dependent on banks, which explains why risks are concentrated there. In TPI's design model, countries shielded themselves from market maladjustments, sparing the banking activity (under the supervision of the ECB), while trying to control inflation.

Fighting Inflation

Discarding the initial 0.25% interest rate hike was the answer to high prices observed for some time. More than impoverishing the population, history had shown time and again that high inflation undermines the usefulness of a currency as a unit of account and as a store of value, also harming long-term investments.

For no other reason, the creation of the inflation targeting regime. Implemented by New Zealand in late 1989, it became a standard tool in the rest of the world for achieving price stability. However, just over three decades later, perhaps the time had come for an update.

Circumstances were quite different, given global debt and savings levels. Furthermore, the world's major economies did not see much benefit in terms of productivity or propensity to save when comparing a 2% inflation target to a 4% inflation target (not applicable, of course, to emerging economies).

Zero Lower Bound

For Europe, a higher inflation target would prevent negative interest rates from being adopted again (they were at -0.50% before the aforementioned ECB meeting).

With a higher target, interest rates, in real terms rather than nominal terms, could be negative, providing the necessary stimulus to the economy without savers withdrawing their funds from banks.

Considering the fuel and food supply shock caused by the war in Ukraine, a higher inflation target would eliminate a dearer financial squeeze, sparing the labor market from a recessive environment.

Financial Innovation

Making the change when prices are at all-time highs could be deadly to any central bank credibility. This explained the search for other alternatives.

As a way of getting around the lack of a transfer mechanism so that member countries could face adverse market conditions, Europe always created its own solutions.

In 2021, Germany and France managed to approve a program ("Next Generation EU" – NGEU) in which the European Union (and not individual countries themselves) would issue bonds to raise funds that would then be directed to countries most affected by the pandemic.

In order to receive this financial aid, each member state had to present reform proposals, as well as meet established climate and digitalization criteria.

Need For Adaptation

Valid until 2026, the NGEU is expected to be renewed, becoming permanent. However, doubts remain about whether it will need some adaptations until then, considering the war in Ukraine and its consequences in terms of inflation.

In any case, if there is one thing that the European Union (EU) has learned in all these years is that a new fund can always be created, even if that means reshuffling resources provided for through its extensive list of laws.

The unanimity obtained by the ECB before the meeting, something difficult in such a heterogeneous group, showed how right the decision was to leave politics, always a tricky subject, outside.

Within the EU, there had always been a clear division: saving countries in the north dreaded the idea of bailing out those in the south, less productive and with looser fiscal policies.

Luckily for them, the cheap euro boosted tourism, which brought hopes of a temporary relief from market jitters.

CHAPTER 15

SUMMER HEATWAVES

Tourism expectations aside, no one counted on the heatwaves that made the European summer the hottest of all times. Needless to say, it brought again the subject of climate change.

Unlike an armed conflict, it is not concentrated in a single region. China, for instance, delayed the planting of wheat, given the floods resulting from an unusual rainfall regime, which compromised the harvest.

Parts of Africa, meanwhile, grappled with the most severe drought in 40 years. What these apparently isolated incidents show is that extreme scenarios can happen, even simultaneously, drastically reducing agricultural productivity.

Expensive Energy And Biofuels

Alternative fuels, such as biofuels, have always been seen as an asset against energy shocks, such as the one faced with the invasion of Ukraine.

With crop failures becoming more common, would it be a case of forcing the reduction of biofuel production so that people may have enough to eat?

The trade-off is not that simple: even if there are no supply constrains in the domestic market, the prices of other commodities also rise due to the substitution effect. In the lack of wheat (one of Ukraine's main exports), people consume rice.

When it comes to decide who gets fed first, there is another equally important dilemma: how much to be spared for animal feed while building safety stocks? The case of Europe is illustrative: 40% of the wheat planted on the continent is used to feed cows, which also produce milk.

How Politics Get In The Way

Mechanisms created to compensate for the carbon released into the atmosphere, despite promoting renewable energy or reforestation projects, do not always follow an economic logic.

The carbon market basically runs on two models: regulated and voluntary. In the regulated market, known as "cap and trade", companies can pollute up to a certain limit (cap), as well as negotiate their permits (trade).

The voluntary market, however, lost its appeal as corporate image became closely linked to companies' presence in Russian territory, brushing aside any tree-hugging ideals.

Additionally, with the increase in prices of agricultural commodities, it became less advantageous to maintain the forest, rather than plant.

Even so, when inputs such as fertilizer and fuel became more expensive, producers raised demand only up to a certain point, given the volatility that these commodities could face under extreme weather conditions, vis-à-vis the increasingly higher cost of financing, as higher interest rates fought a supply shock induced inflation.

Truth be told, the scarcity resulting from the war in Ukraine showed only one side of the hunger in the world.

A total of 23 countries had already restricted their food exports as an attempt to guarantee self-sufficiency, with

80% of the world's population relying on international trade to meet the most basic nutritional needs.

Any more ambitious global plan would only address the problem in the short term for little is known about how to deal with an ever-punishing Mother Nature.

CHAPTER 16

RESILIENT RUSSIA

Two days after the invasion by Russia, the Ukrainian government decided to post the addresses of its bitcoin, ethereum, and tether wallets on social media in order to receive donations.

With its banking activities already reduced, it was a quick and cheap way to raise money while the formal help followed the bureaucratic channels in Brussels and Washington.

The initiative was successful, promoting a series of other actions.

Despite the low values when compared to the aid programs of supranational institutions such as the World Bank, US$ 6.5 million was the amount raised through a non-fungible token (NFT) auction of the Ukrainian flag. Crowdfunding platforms were then launched to buy 3D printers, used to manufacture drone parts.

Ukraine, while not exposed to sanctions, improvised in its war effort. But what about Russia? Six months after the start of the conflict, "Fortress Russia" held up better than expected.

No Police

Some 100 countries, or 40% of the world's GDP, were not strictly following sanctions.

The measures that gained the most attention were

precisely the least effective ones. As much as footages showing oligarchs' asset confiscations were successful on the internet, sanctions against the Russian elite did not influence much Kremlin politics.

Furthermore, telling other countries what to do within their own territories required certain skills, especially when taking into account different legislations and interests.

Not With My Money

What few are aware of is that preventing the transfer of money or halting the trading of assets harms both sides of any transaction.

By excluding Russian banks from the SWIFT messaging system in the first weeks of the war, one of Europe's main financial links was damaged. The German part of the Target 2 system, which settles transactions between eurozone banks, became compromised.

Anyone could argue that the problem would spill over the rest of the continent were it not for the American impetus to boss the world, forbidding US banks of acting as intermediaries for other financial institutions.

Something close to 40% of all cross-border transactions are carried out via blue striped green banknotes, the same ones that facilitate transactions between other less traded currencies.

Why Execution Is Important

If there is one thing that BRICS' countries stockpile is a good variety of top-notch central bankers.

Elvira Nabiullina, responsible for managing the reserves of the Central Bank of Russia, raised interest rates from 9.5%

to 20%, in an aim to contain the ruble's free fall, without giving much thought to the unpopularity of such measure. This allowed interest rates to return to 8% at the end of July (a lower level than before the war), even with the country defaulting on a payment of US$ 100 million owed to foreign bondholders, a consequence of sanctions targeted to the banking sector.

There was, no doubt, an "artificial" value of the rouble, given the capital controls in the country. However, even with unavailable reserves, the country still received a lot from abroad, given how much it exported in fossil fuels.

The oil sector alone accounted for no less than 36% of the Russian budget.

New Markets

Dodging the traps imposed by economic sanctions implied serving other markets, such as China (which had the CIPS payment system and whose currency was conveniently traded on Moscow's exchange) and India.

Both bought Russian oil at a price US$ 25 below the market reference price (Brent), which was still advantageous given that high oil prices ceased to exist in 2014, when the last commodity boom came to an end.

Upgrades

Despite having diversified its economy, much of Putin's country's infrastructure is supplied by foreign technology. Without a flow of new components, there is no way it could maintain and update machinery and equipment, precisely at a time when Russia filled its coffers with an additional US$ 265 billion in oil revenues.

In the absence of suppliers, prohibited of shipping parts

due to sanctions, the only way out was to search elsewhere.

Arab Souk

A neighbor whose currency has devalued by 75% in a period of 4 years could be the solution for a country rich in dollars.

This was the case of Turkey. By becoming a cheap supplier of various goods, as in a typical Arab market, Erdogan favored his re-election, as well as guaranteed hard currency, without having to worry about attracting capital from other parts of the world by raising interest rate.

Therefore, it was possible to maintain abundant credit and stimulate growth.

As much as some European countries tried to soften the impact of higher energy prices six months into the war, recent economic studies pointed out that strategies to cap prices increased consumption, going in the opposite direction of the desired intention, which was to reduce dependency on Russian gas.

Members of the European Union (EU) are served in different ways when it comes to their energy needs and their suppliers, which made any consumption reduction plan coordinated by the European Commission more complex.

While Putin resisted, what was the resolve of the 27 EU member states, considering they had to defend the block's interests above all else?

Contrary to initial expectations, sudden death did not come to Russia.

CHAPTER 17

THE QUEEN AND THE POUND

On September 8th, HM Queen Elizabeth II dies in Balmoral, Scotland, shortly after completing 70 years as the United Kingdom's reigning-monarch (the longest ever).

Other than the fact itself, this brought to light the economic changes that had taken place not only in what was once the British Empire but also its currency, the pound.

The Pound Sterling

It was once the world's main currency.

It left the post sometime between the first and second world wars, when it was replaced by the US dollar. Currently, it is one of the five most traded currencies on the international market, along with the dollar (already mentioned), the euro, the Japanese yen and the Swiss franc.

Unlike its peers, the pound recently had a very volatile performance, more similar to the currencies of emerging economies. It fell more than the euro at the beginning of the pandemic and, since then, had fluctuated mainly due to internal problems in the United Kingdom (UK).

With enough liquidity to change hands at any time, it is not a currency distorted by capital controls (such as in Russia and China), populist policies (such as in Argentina) or macroeconomic experiments (such as in Turkey).

Quite the opposite. Although Great Britain is responsible

for 3% of the world's GDP, close to 10% of all transactions in foreign currencies are based on the pound. Given its importance, what explains this loss of value?

Brexit

On the eve of June 24, 2016, all polls pointed to the "Remain" in the European Union (EU) result. With the unfavorable "Leave" in the next morning, the pound suffered a free fall against other currencies.

Interestingly, a few months later, the British currency fell victim to a "flash crash" during the Asian trading session.

As much as one can blame the role of algorithms in asset trading, which automatically execute orders as prices reach a certain level, other factors, not linked to technology itself, played a greater role.

A Matter Of Trust

How much investors trust a government's ability to quell a crisis is the key question.

Speeches unfavorable to the business environment, not to mention immigration issues, played against the image that London had enjoyed since Margaret Thatcher's era.

For no other reason, that year, the pound sterling made its first appearance among the worst currencies in the world in a ranking compiled by Bloomberg.

Since then, it hasn't recovered, largely due to negotiations with Brussels. Once cut off from the EU, its main market, growth expectations for the UK couldn't be worse. Still, problems are not always home grown.

Leaving The Exchange Rate Mechanism

As every trader knows, the value of a currency (or even its "trend", in Forex parlance), is nothing more than a reflection of its economic fundamentals.

Even before the implementation of the euro, Europe was already conducting some currency experiments. In 1987, the pound entered the so-called European Exchange Rate Mechanism (ERM) where various currencies in the region were pegged to the Deutsche Mark.

With the fall of the Berlin Wall two years later, it became the currency of both sides of Germany (west and east).

As a way of favoring Helmut Kohl's re-election, the Östmark (East Germany's currency) was kept at a higher rate than the Deutsche Mark, albeit at a higher debt cost due to the country's reunification.

Once the election was concluded, the Östmark reached parity (1:1) with the Deutsche Mark. Its massive injection on the eastern side, as the old currency was exchanged for the new one, generated an inflationary movement within the country.

Breaking The Bank Of England

The Bundesbank, which at the same time supported the ERM and conducted monetary policy in Germany, was forced to raise interest rates while other European economies (and England specifically) were in recession.

At that moment, it became clear that the ERM, as conceived, became a secondary objective.

Selling European currencies short, betting that they would not keep their respective prices, became the main strategy traders used to make money and, with the pound sterling, it was no different.

But since authorities never mention the devaluation of any

currency in advance, staying in the game until it actually happened is what set George Soros apart from the rest.

In 1992, the Bank of England (the country's central bank) went bankrupt while trying to defend its currency, which fell from a ratio of 2.95 pounds per Deutsche Mark to 2.50 pounds per Deutsche Mark, generating a profit of US$2 billion for Soros' legendary Quantum Fund.

Queue Of Prime Ministers

Boris Johnson, who promised to "get Brexit done", was the third prime minister to leave in a period of just 6 years.

As in other parts of the world, the UK was experiencing the highest inflation ever, which had led to an endless wave of strikes, in a low growth economic environment.

The dispute between Rishi Sunak, a Stanford alumnus who was previously the finance minister, and Liz Truss, the foreign secretary, focused on the broad range of issues that needed fixing such as:
- Taxation and public spending
- Energy policy
- How to attract investments
- Labor market and new skills

As much as the death of the queen marked the end of an era, movements in the pound reflected the economic and geopolitical changes in the UK.

The worst price reached by the British currency since 1985 showed not only skepticism towards the proposals presented, but also took center stage the role of the United Kingdom, a G7 member, in the world.

CHAPTER 18

NO PRODUCTIVITY

There is no economic growth without productivity. Paul Krugman, winner of the 2008 Nobel Prize in Economics, once quoted well: "Productivity isn't everything, but in the long run it is almost everything."

An increase in productivity, where resources ("labor" and "capital") are put to their best use, is the way to increase incomes and living standards. Hence, the differences in income per capita among countries.

How to leverage this magical element in the economy is more art than science. Nonetheless, it is known that it is a combination of more education, more investments, and the large-scale use of new technologies.

Remote Work

The possibility of remote work (and Zoom meetings) promised productivity gains not seen for a long time. After all, if people could get away from traffic and office distractions, they could also conduct their activities better.

As this experience showed, productivity growth requires new ways of producing goods or offering services, which also implies in closing certain businesses so that resources (always scarce) can be allocated to more promising opportunities.

According to US statistics, productivity had grown at a slower pace for at least a decade, unlike the mid-1990s, when the world integrated into international trade and global supply chains.

With that in mind, is society doomed with a lack of new practical ideas, even with the possibilities offered by artificial intelligence (AI) and cloud computing?

According to Larry Summers, economist and former US Secretary of the Treasury, lack of public policy was to blame. If governments were incapable of provoking an increase in spending and investment, there is no way to generate growth.

This explained the low levels of world GDP in the years leading up to covid-19.

Investing In The Future

If supply increases by means of greater productivity, there is less inflationary pressure (the big economic issue of the year). This statement seemed obvious were it not for a few details.

The benefits of this type of investment are only perceived after a period of 3 to 5 years. This is due to the necessary learning curve until new technologies are used in different sectors of the economy.

As they are incorporated into businesses, they create the so-called "intangible capital", leaving a legacy of knowledge ("know-how") that drives productivity as it becomes more widespread ("Productivity J-curve").

In other words, many mistakes are made until anything becomes standard procedure. But that was not the case for the last 2 years, which explained part of the problem. The "investments" made by companies more recently aimed to guarantee their stocks, due to a great logistics disarray, rather than change the way their businesses worked.

Considered as such in the national accounts, they did not include the inefficiencies generated by the chaos that ensued with the lockdowns. In this environment, funds that were previously kept for research and development (R&D) purposes were redirected to crisis management.

The Recipe

Some time ago, the Organization for Economic Co-operation and Development (OECD) compiled a series of data that led to the publication of the "Future of Productivity".

As a body that formulates guidelines for member countries, the focus on public policies was quite clear, in line with what Larry Summers defended because, if left to private agents, innovations remain concentrated in only a few companies.

In addition to encouraging research, the recommendations for developed financial markets, so that resources would be allocated to the best opportunities, and a legal framework that included bankruptcy adherent to a world where companies try (and fail) until they succeed.

With regards to competition, the reduction of barriers to entry and of labor laws that restrict labor mobility, as well as funding for lifelong learning of current and future workers.

A point that is often ignored, but that was also suggested by the OECD, is the change in the rules of urban planning and development, which make housing costs affordable in large cities, where innovation usually spreads more easily.

Service Sector

The service sector, given the limitations of reaching

a certain scale, was largely favored by post-pandemic innovation. However, greater productivity levels depend on other factors, such as investments in infrastructure and regulation.

While some argue that current technologies are less transformative than those of the past, others say that the way productivity is measured does not capture the increasingly important intangible component of the formula.

Whatever the answer, it is a fact that, in many parts of the world, the population is not only aging, but also decreasing (reduction of the "labor" factor).

Modern societies rotate around logistics, telecommunications and finances, all of which have faced enormous challenges with the pandemic, geopolitical tensions, and higher interest rates across the board.

Work related ills such as "the great resignation" and "quiet quitting" are nothing more than consequences of this phenomenon of low productivity and low growth, where qualifications obtained throughout life do not match the way companies at large operate.

According to the OECD publication, people with a higher qualification than required for the job were more common than the opposite.

CHAPTER 19

REAGANOMICS REVIVAL

High inflation rates and high interest rates.

This was the US scenario in 1981, when Ronald Reagan, a former Hollywood actor, became president of a country already in recession.

To get around the situation, he implemented policies focused on 3 elements, which later became known as Reaganomics:
1. Tax cuts
2. Increases in government spending (including the military budget)
3. Deregulation

At the time, there were serious doubts as to whether economic stimuli were the most appropriate, given the efforts of the Federal Reserve (Fed) to fight inflation with a 19% interest rate. However, as it turned out, Reaganomics worked.

Between the years of 1982 and 1984, domestic demand, which benefited from a greater participation of women in the labor market, grew by around 15% when compared to Japan (5%), and Europe (less than 3%).

Back then, the dollar played a vital role. As it happened in 2022, it strengthened against other currencies, which helped to control inflation as imports became cheaper.

The Least Bad Option

By and large, experienced foreign exchange traders know that the dollar is not the perfect currency to own, but the least bad option when disaster strikes.

This can be explained by two elements:
1. The flight to safety in moments of great uncertainty
2. Portfolio reallocations that take place with each interest rate increase promoted by the Fed.

A scenario in which oil and natural gas prices remain high additionally favors the dollar, as the US became an energy exporting country in 2019 thanks to the shale revolution.

Other Times

President Donald Trump launched his own version in 2018, also taking advantage of the appreciated dollar. As the Fed turned increasingly aggressive, was it the case for a Reaganomics comeback?

In the early 1980s, the dollar appreciated by more than 80% against the currencies of Americas' main trading partners. Along with its robust economy, it brought into its shores huge capital flows from all over the world, creating unwanted external imbalances.

Reagan's economic advisers didn't seem too bothered. They argued that the high interest paid by an international reserve currency attracted capital from anywhere and everywhere, confirming the economic supremacy of the USA.

The first side effects were felt in Latin American countries, which had their foreign loans cut as they joined Mexico in the long default queue.

Currency Manipulation

Things changed after 1985, as protectionism took hold of the American economy. Japan was blamed for the dismantling of local industries (something similar to China's position under Donald Trump).

After approximately 100 protectionist measures were passed by Congress, James Baker, Reagan's Secretary of the Treasury, proposed a plan where, with the help of other countries, the dollar would be devalued.

On September 22, 1985, the Plaza Accord was signed at the Plaza hotel in New York, by the authorities of the US, Japan, Germany, France and England. Over the next 2 years, the desired objective was achieved.

After suffering an accumulated fall of 54% against the German D-mark and the Japanese yen, the time had come for the dollar to stabilize, thus initiating the opposite movement. With a new agreement, called the Louvre Accord, exchange rates were kept within certain bands, not publicly known, by the same countries.

The tactic worked, but also created other imbalances in Europe and Japan.

The Role Of Central Banks

Shielding central banks of these and other political movements was what led to their independence.

The truth is that central banks have been around for a long time. The first, the Swedish central bank, started its activities in 1668. Its main objective was to be the government's lender and, in the case of banking troubles, the lender of last resort.

Inflation and full employment targets, for central banks with a dual mandate, were only incorporated in recent decades.

Taking into account the destabilizing power of climate change, climate targets became a concern, with the expectation that they would be added to central banks' umbrella of supervisory functions such as financial and exchange rate stability.

Experiences with quantitative easing (QE) and negative interest rates since the 2008 crisis, which were adapted to the pandemic years, together with central bank digital currencies (CDBCs) and new geopolitical developments would nonetheless shape their powers and attributions in the future.

How much they will retain of their independence is yet to be seen.

Looking Forward

Concerning Reaganomics itself, the policies adopted by the Reagan administration did not prevent inflation from returning a few years later. The situation was only brought under control when the US Congress approved a tax increase in the following decade, returning to the previous level.

Furthermore, coordinating a currency devaluation or stabilization would be infinitely more difficult today, considering the weight of China, the rules of the European Union and the internal problems faced by the United Kingdom.

To reduce possible imbalances arising from a stronger dollar, certain conditions would have to be met. The first one would be the reduction of the growth gap between the main world powers.

As long as this situation endured, large volumes would still flow to the US, generating further monetary tightening, in a vicious cycle where the contraction of the world economy would lead to new flights to safety and hence, new interest rate hikes by the Fed.

The second, and equally important, depended on how quickly Europe and China would get rid of factors beyond their control (the war and the fight against covid respectively), something that Reagan didn't have to worry about, given the collapse of the Soviet Union in 1991.

CHAPTER 20

INFLATIONARY BUDGETS

Every now and then government spending makes the headlines, whether because of the stimulus given during the pandemic, the issue of increasing inequality or even the risk it poses to the European Union (EU).

Looking forward, other elements may bring additional pressures, such as:

- An aging population, which raises pension and health costs
- A nation that defends itself, increasing its military budget
- A society that cares about climate change, which requires new "green" investments
- An economic bloc that aims self-sufficiency through its own industrial policy

The problem is not so much the isolated impact of each one of them, but their sum over time, diverting resources that could be allocated to productivity, for instance.

Admittedly, the world will work with different rules than those applied during the 1980s. At that time, high inflation and double-digit interest rates were reversed with fiscal and monetary policy moving in the same direction (with the exception of Reaganomics).

In this new arrangement that promises to dominate the global economy, there is a clear conflict between central bankers and their inflation targets and governments whose list of demands only grows.

Higher Inflation Levels

Regardless of the debate on how inflation expectations are formed, it is believed that inflation levels will remain higher.

As much as the expenses incurred by governments in the last 2 years are known, assessing the damage caused by the disruption in the oil and gas markets is not so simple, given the importance of the energy sector in all economic activities.

One way to measure this variable would be the change in wages vis-à-vis the increase in labor productivity. That alone would prove to be a good indicator for higher price levels, all else being equal.

In the mind of any central banker, the greater the difference (or "gap") between wages and productivity, the greater the unemployment rate ("sacrifice") required to bring inflation to levels more consistent with the inflation targeting regime.

Economics Lesson

No matter what fiscal strategy is adopted (more spending or less revenue), when a central bank decides to raise interest rates, the ideal is for public debt to stabilize as a percentage of GDP.

Thomas Sargent, an economist, together with a colleague, published a work in 1981 showing that without this "anchor", increases in interest rates generate more inflation (rather than the opposite effect), as governments borrow more to meet higher interest rate payments.

Other studies confirm this thesis. While many credit Paul

Volcker for the success in fighting inflation in the 1980s, it was only effectively contained when fiscal policy aligned with monetary policy.

New Budget Challenges

That said, how to accommodate the following items that have become quite urgent on budget agendas?

1. NATO target
2. Net-zero infrastructure

Starting with military spending, NATO member countries have a target of 2% of GDP since 2006, but that mark was never achieved before.

With the invasion of Ukraine by Russia, the focus turned back to this subject, with even more aggressive goals, as it was the case of the United Kingdom, grappling with its own budgetary chaos.

This is a cost that, added to an aging population and the decarbonization target, would consume between 2% and 3% of GDP already in the next decade, without increasing the tax burden in the same proportion.

In terms of net-zero, around 90% of the planet has already committed to it.

Technological details aside, the truth is that much of the energy that will make the economy spin will not only increasingly depend on clean sources, but will also require a much more robust infrastructure to handle the demand of everything that is being electrified, such as electric vehicles.

Large projects can benefit from economies of scale and from carbon pricing, were it not for the political agenda.

In the absence of a gradual process for the energy transition, which may even include an industrial policy aimed at regionalization and self-sufficiency, it is more likely that governments will spend a lot and poorly, leaving the bill to society.

Acting Properly

Higher inflation targets would give central banks more leeway to act, reducing interest rates without causing other problems. One thing that the last decade has shown is that it is not always possible to predict the consequences of measures that technically make sense.

When the zero lower bound was breached, as in Europe, savers began to withdraw their funds from banks, undermining monetary policy itself.

On the same token, quantitative easing ("QE"), which was intended to stimulate the economy temporarily, ended up being used for much longer than initially anticipated, inflating the value of every asset in the world (including crypto).

Hence, the biggest challenge is how to maintain credibility when changing a reference that guides all economic activity, whether in regards to prices observed in supermarkets, whether in terms of the impact on futures contracts.

In the meantime, it is up to governments to spend and, at the same time, generate more growth so that the debt/GDP ratio remains at sustainable levels, thus preventing the clash of opposing forces between monetary policy (interest rates as a defense against inflation) and fiscal policy (which began to incorporate new demands).

Time to give up on the terms "hawkish" and "dovish"?

CHAPTER 21

THE SLUMP IN BIG TECH

High-growth stocks suffer when interest rates rise. This dynamic was already known at the beginning of the year, even before the inflationary impacts caused by Russia's invasion of Ukraine. But, considering the digital revolution of the last 2 years, what explained the dismal results of big tech companies?

A closer look indicated that they started to operate more like other traditional sectors. As their revenues declined, they looked for new niches to boost profitability.

With plenty of money, they turned into large and bloated structures, containing business areas that were not necessarily viable, which made dividend distribution difficult. In a period of 5 years, it is a fact that things got worse. The return on invested capital went from over 60% to less than half that amount (26%).

A number of factors contributed to bringing these firms back to Earth.

Governance

Publicly traded technology companies became popular at the expense of a corporate structure where the founder, due to his "vision", kept decision-making powers for himself.

Over the years, this fostered a culture of excess. First, due to the absence of an internal body with enough strength to represent shareholders' interests. Second, by the widespread belief that a founder can repeat the same success formula (as it was the case with Facebook and Meta).

Business Model

Genius aside, the truth is that these companies have some constraints, which limit any future growth potential, starting with the network effect.

The perceived value of a good or service increases as it attracts more users, which explains why so much was spent in the early stages (something that was only possible thanks to the low interest rate environment of the last decade).

Low barriers to entry, the second element of this business model, is a consequence of the free offer and simplicity that guide any and all startup ideas. That said, any social media fad is enough to threaten the position of incumbents, forcing them to spend as well.

Considering the third aspect, the need to be part of a larger infrastructure provided by third parties, that binds them to the rules imposed by others, including the authorities themselves.

Techglomerates

Are the parts alone worth more than the whole? Business books are full of examples of enterprises that lost focus and profitability as they spread to other sectors.

The investments made by big techs turned them into the buried industrial companies of the past. Just like them, they identified the diminishing marginal benefit of their biggest sources of income, putting their money to work elsewhere.

Amazon's case is quite illustrative: the company bet on cloud computing to support its e-commerce. Today, this activity finances acquisitions in sectors as diverse as entertainment and health.

Even smaller companies ventured into the mission of conquering the world, partnering with the proper financing agents.

Private Equity

Private equity entered techs by adapting its medium-sized companies' expertise to venture capital. Over time, it became a credit mall.

As a result, startups postponed plans to go public. If in the 1980s a nascent company waited 8 years to list itself on US stock exchanges, this period increased to 11 years two decades later, meaning most of the gains were kept among a small group of participants.

A world of low interest rates also provided other profitable alternatives. The skill for a certain type of business was replaced by financial engineering's more opportunistic approach. Competing funds transacted with each other, which not necessarily encouraged the creation of new products or services.

Whether they turn into dust as markets adjust to the wake-up call of higher interest rates around the world is yet to be seen. Due to the fact that these funds will eventually sell assets and distribute returns to investors at some point in the future, they are subject to market values substantially lower than those practiced in the past.

As this chapter shows, companies structured with a fairer governance model and better management teams tend to perform better, as it is the case of both Apple and Microsoft. High inflation and higher mortgage rates have dented consumers discretionary purchasing habits, meaning big techs had to work differently.

The private equity industry, always seen as ruthless for its relentless cost-cutting and mass layoffs, gained a following. The only difference is how tech companies do it.

CHAPTER 22

FTX GOES BUST

In November 2021, FTX, the third largest crypto exchange in the world, was valued at US$ 25 billion. It wasn't riding alone. Around the same time, 12 startups exploring blockchain technology had turned into unicorns.

With the price of bitcoin at all-time highs, it was believed that an increasing demand would lead to the regulation of the crypto sector and, hence, to the creation of new service providers.

Cryptoppportunities

In the virtual world, cryptoassets are basically created in 3 ways:
- Decentralized Finance (DeFi), used for financial services;
- Non-fungible tokens (NFTs) for the ownership of digital artworks;
- Cryptocurrencies, offered as rewards in games.

For no other reason, the exchanges' many investments. Coinbase, via its venture capital (VC) arm, bet on various deals while FTX itself joined other companies in order to raise funds for a $100 million gaming fund.

Unlike Big Techs, which were nurtured in Silicon Valley, the race for crypto wealth was on a global scale.

Cryptolobby

With so much money flowing in one direction, it's would be expected that governments would want to control or even tax it in some way. In Europe and the US specifically, it became common practice to hire people with a minimum government experience for the purpose of lobbying.

Even companies with few resources and no innovative strategy sought means to defend their interests via industry associations. If rules are unavoidable, then better to "help shape them", especially with the ones that serve to protect small investors.

Among the guidelines defended by exchanges and other participants, self-regulation and the creation of a specific body for the crypto world. To press ahead and get the attention of congressmen, bitcoins were distributed.

Cryptolosses

With the end of cheap money in the world, some purge was imagined among companies with weak fundamentals. Still, it was expected that players themselves would take the initiative to keep things running.

As much as they demonstrated financial capacity, it is a fact that containing withdrawal requests is hard. FTX had to honor $650 million in a single day.

If a business runs into trouble, what about its token, which in theory should distribute part of the profits to its holders? With the panic that set in, FTX's token lost 90% of its value and that is not the end of the story.

As with any banking crisis, when a major institution fails, it is just a matter of time before its business partners meet the same fate. The FTX empire alone (FTX global and FTX.US, in addition to the crypto fund Alameda Research) incentivized the exchange of tokens as collateral for loans.

Cryptoleverage

Through leverage, it favored speculation and some very risky bets by using both its assets as well as third-party assets deposited on exchanges, which boosted the value of its own tokens as trading volume increased, since agents have no tool to evaluate prices.

Unlike traditional assets, cryptos pay no interest, dividends or income, and are still exposed to hackers. Furthermore, in a world of higher interest rates, many of these virtual instruments, used to lend money, are forced into ever riskier operations.

When the worse happens, there is no "crypto central bank" to offer a minimum of order and liquidity. Without some form of deposit insurance, the money is simply gone, meaning that Sam Bankman-Fried, founder of FTX and son of Stanford University law professors, went bankrupt.

The Human Factor

Sam was anything but a crypto scammer. Impressed by the wonders of technology, he believed in his great project. Aware of the dedication that a 24/7 market requires, he slept next to his desk.

Altruistic, he planned to donate his fortune when not using it to rescue other companies or fight for the proper regulation. FTX went down for the same reasons as always: greed and fear of its 5 million users, no matter how brilliant and selfless its founder.

When something goes wrong, the blame game starts. For his defense, Sam hired Michael Milken's (the 80's "junk bond king") lawyer. Markets evolve and mature, but people, unfortunately, do not.

CHAPTER 23

THE FUTURE

What to expect of 2023? If inflation was the big issue of 2022, recession might just as well be next year's main topic. Central bankers are still figuring out the best way to fight the consequences of a series of supply shocks that have taken place since the pandemic. A generalized sense of instability, whether caused by geopolitical reasons or even extreme climate conditions, makes for a strong case when setting prices higher, as if economic agents impose an "uncertainty spread".

Due to this, they remain limited in their ability to discern how prices behave and for how long. Will the 2% target still be pursued or is a higher, albeit stable, inflation better suited for a world where debts levels are higher for governments, companies, and households alike?

Truth be told, monetary policy will not reestablish global oil and gas markets, fix macroeconomic inconsistencies or make the climate milder. Additionally, inflation can't be fought without any efforts in terms of productivity, not to mention some fiscal discipline.

As credit becomes more restrictive, borrowing is no longer the answer for squeezed budgets as economies dive into downturns. Destruction of demand replaces stimulus for more demand.

Sure enough, the road ahead remains bumpy as next year starts with new vocabulary: "permacrisis", the junction of

"permanent" and "crisis".
Better buckle up!

NOHAD TOUFIC HARATI

All rights reserved.

ABOUT THE AUTHOR

Nohad T. Harati

NOHAD T. HARATI has a degree in business administration in addition to both an MBA in finances and an LLM in financial market law from a prestigious Brazilian educational institution (Insper).

She started her career at a local commodities broker, becoming a private banking investment analyst for a Swiss financial institution a few years later.

She also participated as an alternate board member at Companhia Energética de Minas Gerais (CEMIG), a Brazilian energy distribution company.

Currently, she manages a proprietary portfolio, runs a family office and is a regular columnist for the Brazilian investment startup Mais Retorno (https://maisretorno.com/portal/autor/nohadharati) in addition to publishing articles in her own personal pages:

LinkedIn: https://www.linkedin.com/in/nohadharati/
Quora (English): https://www.quora.com/profile/Nohad-Harati
Quora (Portuguese): https://pt.quora.com/profile/Nohad-Harati

www.ingramcontent.com/pod-product-compliance
Lightning Source LLC
Chambersburg PA
CBHW070257220526
45465CB00004B/1639